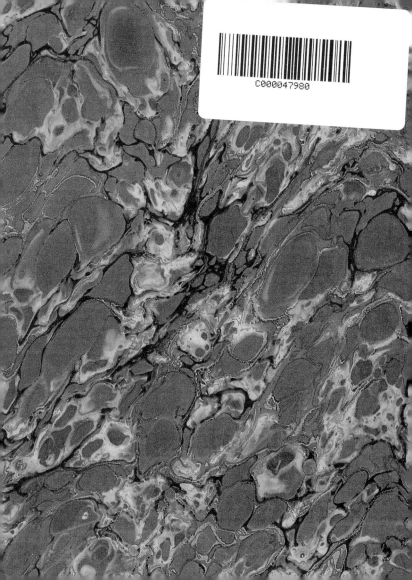

THE 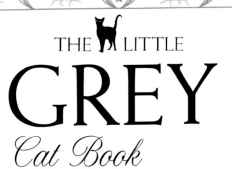 LITTLE

GREY

Cat Book

ELIZABETH MARTYN
DAVID TAYLOR

DORLING KINDERSLEY
London · New York · Stuttgart

A DORLING KINDERSLEY BOOK

PROJECT EDITOR Candida Ross-Macdonald
DESIGNER Camilla Fox
MANAGING EDITOR Krystyna Mayer
MANAGING ART EDITOR Derek Coombes
PRODUCTION Lauren Britton

First published in Great Britain in 1993 by
Dorling Kindersley Limited, 9 Henrietta Street, London WC2E 8PS

A CIP catalogue record for this book is available
from the British Library

ISBN 0-7513-0040-3

Reproduced by Colourscan, Singapore
Printed and bound in Hong Kong by Imago

CONTENTS

SHADOWY
Cat

*Grey cats, both real
and imaginary, that
have refused to fade
into the twilight.*

HALL OF FELINE FAME

Elegant grey cats have been chosen as companions to
the famous and celebrated in all walks of life.

Who could resist a grey cat?
There is something elegant in
that cloud-coloured coat that
never loses its appeal.

MEWSES
Sir Walter
Scott, poet
and novelist,
was devoted
to his grey
tabby, Hinx.
The cat ruled
the family
bloodhounds
with a rod of
iron: every
evening the
tyrannical cat
would sit by
the door and
cuff the dogs'
ears as they
went past.
Hinx got his
come-uppance after 15 years of
unchallenged authority, when a
rebellious puppy bit back –
with fatal results.

Cats feature in the works of
Nobel Prize winner Doris
Lessing. As a child, the author
had a blue-grey Persian. When
the cat died,
she swore that
it could not
be replaced,
but years
later, friends
gave her a
tabby-Siamese
cross kitten
that captured
her heart
again. The
"exotically
beautiful
beast" was
simply named
Grey Cat.
Another great
author with a
penchant for
cats was
Samuel Johnson. As well as the
fêted Hodge, the lexicographer
owned Lily, a small, sweet-
natured grey cat.

Left: Doris Lessing with feline friend
Right: Sir Walter and a smug Hinx
Below: Queen Victoria, a patron of gorgeous greys

ROYAL AND SAINTLY PATRONS

Queen Victoria attended the first major English cat show in 1871. Among the rare and beautiful breeds was an elegant grey Persian. The delectable cat so inspired the Queen that she acquired two Blue Longhairs of her own, and became patron of the Blue Persian Society.

On a more ascetic note, the theologian St. Jerome, who translated the scriptures from Greek into Latin, also owned a grey cat. He has been portrayed by both Albrecht Dürer and Antonello da Messina at work in his study with a small grey cat. It is said that if a cat has been lost, a prayer to St. Jerome may help to find it.

HALL OF FICTION

Grey has always been a favourite colour of cat creators, with several cartoon cats sporting grey coats.

The most famous cat-and-mouse duo are Tom and Jerry, created by Hanna and Barbera. Tom's eternal pursuit of Jerry won them seven Oscars. They reached their peak in the 1940s and early 1950s, even taking a swim with star Esther Williams in the film *Dangerous When Wet*. In the 1960s, Hanna and Barbera created Top Cat, a very different character. For all his mad, bad, and dangerous-to-know image, Tom lived an easy suburban life. "TC" made his home in downtown dustbins and lived by charm and his wits.

DISNEY DEBUT

Walt Disney cartoons were dominated for years by mice, ducks, and dogs. Cats only had supporting roles – for example, Willow, a grey tabby, helped to thwart the evil Cruella de Vil in *101 Dalmatians*. Then, in 1970, came *The Aristocats* – a feature-length cat cartoon. The male lead was O'Malley, a handsome grey alley cat with winning ways. Charming cinema audiences, he became the consort of Duchess – an elegant white queen – and protector of her trio of kittens, named Berlioz, Toulouse, and Marie.

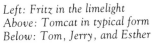

Left: Fritz in the limelight
Above: Tomcat in typical form
Below: Tom, Jerry, and Esther

WILD CATS

A far cry from the innocent world of children's cartoons was Fritz. A louche character who started life in a magazine, Fritz hit the big screen in a cartoon billed as "totally, absolutely and unashamedly unsuitable for children".

Another grey cat you wouldn't cuddle is Tomcat, emblem of the fighter plane of the same name. Tomcat appears on a variety of badges, sometimes disguised as Ali Baba, or a knight, or a Japanese warrior, but always with a far-from-military smirk.

GALLERY OF

Cats

*Beautiful cats of
charm and distinction,
a feast for the eyes in
every imaginable
shade of grey.*

FELINE FEATURES

From the serene charm of the Longhair to the svelte grace of the Oriental, the range of grey cats encompasses a feast of feline good looks, each with its own individual appeal.

NORWEGIAN FOREST CAT
Smoke

BALINESE
Seal Tortie Point

RUSSIAN BLUE

TIFFANY
Black-tipped

KORAT

LILAC LONGHAIR

NON-PEDIGREE
SHORTHAIR

BRITISH BLUE-
CREAM

ABYSSINIAN
Silver

ORIENTAL
Blue Tabby

SHADES OF GREY

Grey cats are prized for their rarity among the more common black-and-white, ginger, or brown tabby colouring of their feline friends. Choose your favourite from soft, silky, thistledown fur or densely piled velvet plush, each one supremely strokable. There are myriad shades, from misty palest silver to sophisticated tones of blue and lilac.

BALINESE
Lilac Point

BRITISH SILVER
TABBY

SILVER TABBY
LONGHAIR

ORIENTAL
*Chocolate Silver
Tabby*

BLUE TABBY
LONGHAIR

ABYSSINIAN
Silver

NON-PEDIGREE
LONGHAIR

ANGORA
Blue-cream

BLUE-CREAM
LONGHAIR

CORNISH REX
*Blue-cream
Smoke*

ABYSSINIAN
Blue-cream

ORIENTAL
Lilac Tabby

MAINE COON
*Blue Tortie Silver
Tabby*

BRITISH BLUE

With a coat like velvet and piercing eyes of copper or orange, this cat turns heads wherever it goes. First created in the late 19th century, the breed declined in this century and was revived in the 1950s. Superb cloud-grey, plush fur gives this cat its enduring appeal and popularity.

Solemn Stare

Those penetrating eyes should be large and round. Another cat with a blue coat and orange eyes is the Chartreux, given its own class in North America, but judged in the same class as a British Blue in Britain.

Cateristics

🐾

Clever and cheeky personality

🐾

Grows deeply attached to its owners

🐾

Faint tabby markings are visible at birth but fade in time

Blue Study

Everything about the British Blue is true to its name, including the nose and paw pads, which should have no hint of pink. This cat is exceptionally affectionate, and makes an excellent pet. It doesn't enjoy excitement, preferring a quiet life.

Built to Last

The cobby, muscular body, the short legs, and the large, round paws of the British Blue give away its street-cat origins. The head should be round and wide, with a short, straight nose. The chin is firm and well developed, and the ears have curved tips.

PEWTER LONGHAIR

The tipping of the Pewter's luxuriant coat makes it look rather like a Chinchilla, and Chinchillas were among its ancestors. Its eyes give the game away, however – rather than green, they are luminous orange or copper, like the eyes of the Blues and Blacks that were its other forebears. The Pewter's body is also more cobby than that of the Chinchilla. The long, abundant coat reaches almost to the paws, and the neck ruff should be full and fall in a deep fringe over the chest. A magnificent plumy tale completes the picture of this attractive feline.

*G*OLDEN *G*LOW
The eyes are large and round, with a rim of black to give them depth and sparkle.

*L*IGHT AND *S*HADE
A shadow-like sprinkling of black over the head, back, legs, and tail gives the appearance of a pewter-grey veil flung over the white coat.

CATERISTICS

Calm and unflappable

Very affectionate; adores being stroked

Superb coat hides a chunky build

FRILLY FRONT
The deep chest frill is white, with less tipping than the rest of the body.

RUSSIAN BLUE

Despite its name, the birthplace of this breed is uncertain. Over the centuries it has been known as the Archangel Cat, the Spanish Cat, and the Maltese Cat, and it is also common in Sweden. An elegant cat, it has an athlete's body, with slender legs and dainty paws. The coat is what makes this cat super-special, however: extremely dense and soft, with a silken shine, it stands away from the body, offering an open invitation to caress.

Relaxing Companion
Calm and obliging, Russian Blues have very quiet voices and are perfectly happy to spend their lives indoors. The elegant, wedge-shaped head with its full whisker pads gives the cat an aloof look.

*T*URNCOAT

In kittenhood, the
Russian Blue has a
fluffy coat, which may
show faint tabby markings.
The evenly coloured blue coat
develops as the cat grows into a
svelte adult.

*P*OLISHED UP

The distinctive double coat
requires just an occasional
brushing followed by a gentle
polishing with a chamois cloth.

*C*ATERISTICS

Shy and retiring
personality

Even blue colour,
with a distinctive
silvery sheen

Considered to be a
lucky omen in Russia

BRITISH SILVER SPOTTED TABBY

This coat has been known for centuries, and examples of it appear in Ancient Egyptian wall paintings. A variation of the mackerel tabby pattern, the markings are broken down from stripes into numerous spots. The coat is silver-grey, overlaid with oval, round, or rosette-shaped spots of jet-black, which should stand out distinctly. The overall effect is streets ahead of the common-or-garden tabby coat.

Unfortunately, this marvellous coat also makes the cat a target for thieves.

Cateristics

🐾

A gentle, friendly breed

🐾

Has the typical tabby
M-shaped marking over
the nose

🐾

Coat is fine, dense, and
very strokable

Face Facts

The eyes are edged with black, and
may be pure green or have a touch of
brown that gives a hazel colour. The
face is broad with a strong chin, and
the short, straight nose is tipped with
a black or brick-red nosepad.

Wild Looks

Although it looks like
its wild cat ancestor,
the British Silver
Spotted is charming
and affable, with
a pleasant nature
and an even
temperament.
Stroking that
gorgeous coat is
very soothing.

Body Beautiful

The British Silver Spotted has
the muscular body typical of
British cats.

BRITISH BLUE-CREAM

This extremely pretty cat is produced by interbreeding Blues with Creams. Breeders also sometimes use Tortoiseshells, and the Blue-cream, like the Tortoiseshell, is a female-only breed. No male kittens are known to have survived into adulthood, and any that did would be sterile. The palest tones of blue and cream are preferred, and there should be no traces of red or white, or of tabby markings. The blue hairs tend to be coarser than the cream, and the coat needs regular grooming, especially in the moulting season, to sift out any fine, loose hairs.

Subtle Shading

The standards for this cat differ across the world: the American calls for patches in a blue-cream background, the British and Australian for intermingled colours with no prominent patches or facial blaze. Kittens may be born blue, the cream appearing as the cat grows up.

Glorious golden or
amber eyes

Lively, curious, and
always interested in
what's going on

Cobby, with sturdy legs
and a short, thick tail

D EEPEST P LUSH
The velvety sheen of the coat looks invitingly
soft. The texture is thick and plush, and the
short fur shows off this breed's muscular body
to perfection. Plenty of stroking will bring up
the coat's natural shine.

L ILAC L ATECOMER
The Lilac is a recent and eye-
catching British breed, derived
from the Lilac Longhair. Its coat
is pinkish-grey with a silver
sheen, and its build is similar to
that of other British cats.

BURMILLA

The Burmilla is a new and beautiful breed, first seen in 1981. It was the fortuitous offspring of a Burmese and a Chinchilla, both belonging to Baroness Miranda von Kirchberg. The kittens had the best of both breeds: the body shape of the Burmese and a coat with all the softness and subtle tipping of the Chinchilla. A truly appealing puss, which deserves to achieve lasting success both as a show cat and as a family pet.

*T*IPPED FOR THE *T*OP

A light, even powdering of black on the silver fur produces a coat of distinction. Vestiges of tabby markings can be seen on the face, ears, tail, legs, and paws.

*C*ATERISTICS

🐈

An even-tempered cat that rarely gets angry

🐈

Short coat is dense and ultra-soft

🐈

Glorious green eyes with dark rims

*S*UMPTUOUS *R*UFF

The first generation of kittens from a Burmese-Chinchilla cross may have a longer coat than is considered ideal for the Burmilla. Although it would not be successful as a show cat, this delightful, soft-coated variation is still a very attractive proposition as a household pet.

*M*OTHER *L*OVE

A Burmilla mother looks affectionately at the Birman kitten she fostered. Both of these breeds have amiable and even-tempered dispositions, and make excellent pets.

BLUE BURMESE

On record as inhabitants of Burmese Buddhist temples as long ago as the 15th century, these cats were once known as "Rajahs". The present-day breed can be traced back to a mating in 1930 between a Siamese and a brown female cat from Burma called Wong Mau. Of heavier build than the Siamese, the Burmese has a uniformly coloured coat without contrasting points. Burmese are very popular for their intelligence, as well as for their glossy good looks. They are gregarious cats, and love people.

CATERISTICS

🐈

A short coat with a deep,
satiny sheen

🐈

Adores being in the
company of humans

🐈

Highly intelligent and
extrovert personality

CHEEKY KITTENS

*Kittens of this breed
are particularly bright
and playful. Burmese
behave well with
children, and the
more attention they
get, the happier they
are. It is best to get
two kittens if you are
out a lot, as the
Burmese languishes
when left to its own
devices for very long.*

EASY-CARE CAT

The steady, intense
gaze of the Burmese is
enhanced by its
slanted eyes. The
short coat needs very
little grooming to keep
its lustrous sheen.
Occasional combing
deals with dead hairs,
while plenty of hand
stroking helps to keep
the coat shiny, as well
as being a positive
pleasure for both cat
and owner.

OUT AND ABOUT

The Blue Tortoiseshell is one of
many varieties. The Burmese has the
outgoing nature of the Siamese, but it
is less vocal and seldom destructive.
Burmese may wander if allowed total
freedom, so some restrictions may
be essential.

KORAT

At home in Thailand, where it originated on the Korat Plateau, this breed plays an important part in traditional custom and is believed to bring good luck. A pair of Korats given to a bride on her wedding day ensure an affluent and happy marriage. The Korat has a thick, smooth coat of blue-grey with a silvery sheen and no hint of stripes or shading. The face is heart-shaped with large ears, and the cat gives a riveting green gaze from eyes that shine "like dewdrops on a lotus leaf", according to verses in the *Cat-Book Poems*, an Oriental book of feline praise written between 1350 and 1767. While Thai cats such as the Siamese have been greatly changed by modern breeding, the Korat remains true to its centuries-old description in this book.

GOOD FRIENDS
Korats get on well with each other, and can settle down with other cats and even with a docile dog, if introduced to each other over time.

JUMP TO IT
Korats enjoy
play: boisterous
games will prove
firm favourites.
However, surprises
such as sudden, loud
noises can easily
startle them.

CATERISTICS

Exceptionally gentle;
good with children

An ancient breed,
little changed over the
passing centuries

Born with golden eyes
that turn green

STROKED WITH SILK
Polishing the fur with silk
enhances the shine that
earned the Korat the name
"cloud-coloured
cat" in its
homeland.

GREY LONGHAIRED NON-PEDIGREE

Although luscious looks are often thought of as being the exclusive property of pedigree felines, there are many domestic non-pedigrees who sport the same glamorous silken fur in equally elegant shades. If you fancy the idea of a friendly and fluffy pet, a longhaired moggie will have masses of charm at a fraction of the price you would pay for a pedigree. Longhaired cats tend to be calmer and more placid than shorthaired ones, and usually adapt well to a life indoors. A thorough grooming every day is a must, but apart from that a longhaired cat needs no special care: just the love and attention that all cats deserve.

*E*LEGANT *A*IR
This sophisticated silver-and-white cat looks rather like a Pewter Longhair, and although its coat is shorter, it is clearly no poor relation.

Blue Boy

This kitten absorbed in play has a coat of pure blue, yet his mother was tortoiseshell. That elusive tail keeps trying to escape ...

Cateristics

❧

Gentle personalities, less rumbustious than their shorthaired counterparts

❧

Come in any number of shades and markings

❧

Fur varies from medium to long and bushy, but is always soft and strokable

Touch of Tabby

Many cross-bred cats show tabby markings somewhere on their bodies, most obvious here on the legs. This is because tabby genes are dominant, and their patterning makes up the basic feline coat. Splashes of white on the face and chest add a delightful touch of character, and contrast well with the even tipping over the rest of the coat.

MYSTIC
Cat

*Choosing the perfect
name for your cat, and
a Zodiac guide to
feline character.*

NAMES AND NAMING

When presented with a tabby-Siamese grey cat, even author Doris Lessing had problems finding a name. She recorded the names she tried – "Melissa and Franny; Marilyn and Sappho; Circe and Ayesha and Suzette" – none of which suited the fabulous feline well enough to stick. To help you out of similar problems, here are some suggestions to suit cats of all shades of grey, from palest mist to darkest granite.

AGNES *After Agnes Grey, the modest and gentle heroine of Anne Bronte's novel; a name suitable for a demure cat.*

ARCHANGEL *A remote port, icebound in winter, and believed to be the original birthplace of the Russian Blue.*

BERGAMOT *The essential oil extracted from this pear-shaped Asian fruit is used to perfume and flavour Earl Grey tea.*

CHARTREUSE *A famous monastery near Grenoble where the monks began breeding blue cats in 1558.*

CHIAROSCURO *Monochrome painting, using only shades of light and dark. A dramatic name for a blotched cat.*

COBWEB *For a fairy-footed cat that could step on a spider's web without breaking it.*

CUMULUS *For a longhaired cat with an abundant, fluffy coat, like a billowing grey cloud.*

ELEGY *After the English 18th-century poet Thomas Grey's celebrated poem, "Elegy Written in a Country Churchyard".*

LADY JANE *Queen of England for just nine days in 1554, the young Lady Jane Grey was rapidly ousted from the throne, imprisoned, and executed.*

MUDLARK *A name given to street urchins. For a cheeky cat that hates having to stay indoors.*

LAVENDER *A cottage-garden shrub with mauve-blue flowers and grey foliage, grown for its strong perfume.*

WILLOW *The grey tabby cat in 101 Dalmatians. A name for a cat with soft grey paws like pussy-willow.*

CAT STARS

Your cat's personality revealed in the heavens.

ARIES
21 MARCH – 20 APRIL
Arien cats never learn to look before they leap: these are the impulsive cats that get stuck in trees or on rooftops. Fiercely devoted to their owners, they make vociferous demands for love and affection.
Food fads: Likes lots of flavour.

TAURUS
21 APRIL – 21 MAY
Patient and persistent, Taurean cats will spend hours working out how to open the cupboard where their food is kept. An indulgent sign, addicted to comfort, with a quiet voice and gentle, loving manner.
Food fads: Seedless grapes, served peeled.

GEMINI
22 MAY – 21 JUNE
Easily bored, Geminian cats need lots of toys and regular playtimes. Always eager to communicate, they find clever ways to make themselves understood. They can be nervous and are easily startled by sudden noises.
Food fads: Chopped nuts to crunch on.

CANCER
22 JUNE – 22 JULY

Cats born under this sign are ultra-intuitive and very quick to pick up any change of atmosphere in their home surroundings. Loyal and loving pets, they are at their happiest when in the midst of family life.
Food fads: A saucer of creamy milk.

LEO
23 JULY – 23 AUGUST

Outwardly confident, Leo cats are more sensitive than they seem, and take a telling-off very much to heart. This sign needs to stay active and Leos may lapse into depression if under-stimulated.
Food fads: A trickle of honey to lick up.

VIRGO
24 AUGUST – 22 SEPTEMBER

Never pushy, Virgoan cats can find it hard to form close relationships, since they fear rejection. Although they are clever, their needs are simple: a comfortable home, an understanding owner, and a reliable routine.
Food fads: Potatoes, mashed with butter.

*L*IBRA
23 SEPTEMBER – 23 OCTOBER

Libran cats dread loneliness and won't let you out of their sight if they can possibly help it. Easygoing creatures, they fit happily into the household and enjoy watching the comings and goings of the family.
Food fads: A slice or two of strawberry.

*S*CORPIO
24 OCTOBER – 22 NOVEMBER

It is important to provide an outlet for the Scorpio cat's energy: if this sign becomes frustrated it can wreak havoc! Scorpios hanker for steadfast love and will grow passionately attached to a caring owner.
Food fads: Flavoursome foods, nothing bland.

*S*AGITTARIUS
23 NOVEMBER – 21 DECEMBER

Boisterous cats that just can't sit still, Sagittarians need a calming influence when they start acting like whirlwinds. They love life and wholeheartedly enjoy stalking their shadows or chasing the cat next door.
Food fads: Fond of herbs, especially sage.

Capricorn
22 DECEMBER – 20 JANUARY
Cats born under this sign can lack self-confidence and may need reassurance before venturing into the company of strangers. They often hide a delightful sense of humour beneath a serious surface.
Food fads: Pasta bolognaise.

Aquarius
21 JANUARY – 18 FEBRUARY
Cool customers, Aquarian cats prefer to walk by themselves and shun close human attachment. This is not to say that they are unfriendly, but they always put their strong desire for independence first.
Food fads: A little chopped kiwi fruit.

Pisces
19 FEBRUARY – 20 MARCH
Piscean pets love their owners to pieces. You can do no wrong in the eyes of this sign. Your Piscean cat can also be relied on to listen and purr soothingly whenever you want to pour out your troubles.
Food fads: Fish, fish, and more fish.

PAMPERED
Cat

*All you need to know to
choose and cherish
your grey cat.*

CHOOSING A CAT

Pets have needs that are every bit as important as yours, so you should think carefully before you invite a new cat into your home.

WHAT SORT OF CAT?

Kittens are adorable, but take a lot of looking after when tiny. They are also highly energetic. Choose a kitten only if you have plenty of time to play with it and can arrange for it to be given three meals a day. Older cats may take time to settle in, but need less one-to-one attention from their owners. Pedigree cats have distinction and good looks, but they can be very expensive, and there may be a waiting list for kittens. Non-pedigrees can have just as much charm, and are less likely to be the targets of cat thieves. In either case, choose a longhaired cat only if you are willing to groom it every day.

POINTS TO CHECK

These are some of the points to consider when you choose your feline friend.

1 Go to a humane society or breeder, not a pet shop.

2 Look for a well-groomed cat with no skin problems or blemishes, and no sign of fleas.

3 Check for bright eyes, clean ears, and sound teeth: these signs indicate a healthy cat.

4 Pick a lively cat that likes being handled. Avoid listless or overly timid cats.

5 Make sure your cat has been given all the necessary vaccinations, and don't take a kitten home if it is under ten weeks old.

CURIOUS CAT
Both adult cats and kittens will explore. Move fragile possessions out of harm's way before you bring a cat home.

PLAYTIME
Provide a few simple toys, and you'll have hours of fun watching your new kitten stalk them across the room.

WELL BROUGHT UP
Kittens are bright and quick to learn, so speak firmly to your new kitten when it is being naughty, and praise it lavishly when it is on its best behaviour.

CAT GLAMOUR

Every grey cat likes to show off its cloudy coat. Longhaired cats need daily attention to keep them fabulously fluffy, but owners of shorthairs should also give puss the pleasure of frequent grooming. Most cats adore being brushed, combed, and generally fussed over, so it is a therapeutic pastime for cat and owner alike.

GROOMING GEAR

Use a soft, bristle brush, which won't create static or break hairs. You will also need a fine-toothed comb for tangles.

GROOMING GUIDE

1 Using a fine-toothed comb, work over the cat's body to remove dead hairs and dirt.

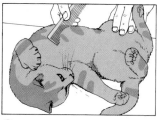

2 Don't forget to comb the tummy. Some cats are very sensitive here, so be gentle.

Claw Tips

When trimming claws, take care to
avoid the pink quick inside, cutting
the white tip only. If in doubt,
ask your vet for a
demonstration.

Bathing Beauty

If your cat gets very
dirty, give it a bath.
Use warm, not hot,
water, and a baby
shampoo. Enlist some
help if possible, and close
doors and windows before
you start. Finish with a
warm towel and keep
kitty indoors until
completely dry.

3 Brush the coat in the
direction of growth. Don't
forget the legs, tail, and head.

4 For the final touch, buff
with a silk or velvet cloth or
a chamois leather to give a gloss.

MEALTIME TREATS

Add variety to your cat's everyday diet by cooking up
a special little treat to tempt the palate. Many foods
are suitable for cats, so have fun experimenting to see
which are your cat's favourites. Make sure fresh water
is always available – this is particularly important if
you feed your cat any dry food.

Breakfast Special

*Place a fresh, free-range egg in
boiling water and cook for four
minutes. Plunge into cold
water to cool, peel off shell,
and mash the egg, mixing the
white well with the yolk. Serve
sprinkled with tiny squares of
wholemeal toast.*

Cheesy Pasta

*Make a white sauce with flour,
butter, and milk and stir in finely
grated cheese to taste. Stir until
smooth. Add cooked, chopped
wholewheat spaghetti or pasta
shapes and a little finely
chopped steamed leek. Allow
to cool before serving.*

Tasty Turkey

Mix cooked turkey meat, cut into small cubes, with cooked rice. Moisten with stock or gravy and serve slightly warm.

Pizza Sensation

Cut a slice of pizza into squares. Toppings can include vegetables, fish, and meat. Avoid salami or anchovy, which can be very salty.

Salad Bowl

Finely grate one-third of a raw courgette and one-third of a raw carrot. Mix together and sprinkle with sesame seeds.

Chicken Liver Risotto

Cook chopped chicken liver for ten minutes in a flavoured stock. Stir into boiled rice and sprinkle with chopped mint or parsley.

Quayside Treat

Poach a small fillet of cod or plaice in fresh milk. Remove all bones and flake fish. Make a tomato sauce, and stir in the poached fish and a little cooked rice.

Juicy Fruit

Scoop small balls of flesh from a ripe melon. Mix with peeled, halved orange segments and a few grapes, peeled and cut into quarters, with their pips removed.

My Cat's Personal Record

Name . . . .

Date of birth . . . . Sex . . . .

Breed . . . .

Coat . . . .

Markings . . . .

Colour of eyes . . . .

Star sign . . . .

How I came to have my grey cat . . . .

. . . .

Vocabulary (list sounds and interpretations). . . . .

. . . .

. . . .

Body language (describe movements and meanings). . . . .

. . . .

Favourite foods and drinks . . . .

. . . .

Best place to stroke . . . .

. . . .

Feline friends . . . .

. . . .

Special people . . . .

. . . .

Cosiest bed . . . .

Sunniest spot . . . .

Things that frighten my cat . . . .

. . . .

Most exciting game . . . .

. . . .

Attention-grabbing ploys . . . .

. . . .

Cleverest tricks . . . .

. . . .

Most memorable moments . . . .

. . . .

A-Z OF CAT CARE

A IS FOR ACCIDENTS

If possible, avoid moving an injured cat. If you have to, use a blanket held taut as a stretcher. Keep the cat warm and do not give anything by mouth. Contact a vet immediately, even if there is no external sign of injury to the cat, because there may be internal damage that is not obvious to you.

B IS FOR BEDTIME ROUTINE

Start in kittenhood for undisturbed nights. Place the cat in its own bed, in a darkened room, with water and a litter tray nearby. Keep the door closed to prevent nocturnal wanderings.

C IS FOR CHILDREN

Teach children to handle cats gently and try to prevent chasing or tail-tugging. Don't let young children lift puss: an insecure cat may bite or scratch trying to get free.

D IS FOR DEAFNESS

Fairly common in old age. A deaf cat must be kept indoors, since it will not be able to hear traffic or other dangers. Consult a vet: the problem may be a treatable build-up of wax in the ear.

E IS FOR EYES

To apply ointment, hold tube parallel to eye and squeeze a line of ointment across eyeball. Gently hold eye shut for ten seconds.

F IS FOR FLEAS

Black specks in the coat and excessive scratching are sure signs of fleas. Treat with powder or spray. Aerosols are more effective, but the sound frightens many cats.

G IS FOR GOING OUT

Every cat relishes the chance to explore the world outside. A lockable cat flap ensures that puss can come and go at will during the day, but can also be kept in safely at night. Give your cat a collar, and attach a tag with both your address and your telephone number engraved on it.

H IS FOR HAIRBALLS

Often a problem for longhaired breeds. All cats will inevitably swallow some fur while they are grooming themselves, but most can regurgitate it without difficulty. If you suspect your cat has a problem, consult a vet, who can prescribe an easily administered lubricant remedy.

I IS FOR ILLNESS

If your cat is ill and needs nursing at home, provide a warm, comfortable bed and keep puss indoors until fully recovered. Feed light but nourishing meals regularly, and ensure that your cat takes liquid – by spoon, if necessary – even if solids are refused.

J IS FOR JITTERS

Living with a very nervous cat can make the whole family jumpy. To calm your pet, try securing it in a large pen where it can feel safe while observing the household noise and bustle, but cannot run away. In time, the cat will realize that there is nothing to fear.

K IS FOR KITTENS

Introduce them to the household gradually, and keep other pets away until they have had a chance to settle down in their new environment.

L IS FOR LOSS OF APPETITE

Sickness is not the only cause. Any upsets, such as moving house, unappetising food, or hot weather, can put puss off eating. Rule these out first.

M IS FOR MILK

Not necessary for nutrition if your cat has a balanced diet, and some cats can have trouble digesting the lactose in it. Make sure that you always provide plenty of fresh water to drink instead.

N IS FOR NUTRITION

Feed your cat a varied diet. Cooked meat, fish, offal, poultry, and rabbit are all excellent sources of protein, but remember to remove any small bones before serving. Many cats also like cheese, another good source of protein. Limit your cat's intake of eggs to two a week, and serve them cooked. Toast, cereals, or pasta add bulk to the diet, but should form no more than one-third of any meal.

O IS FOR OBESITY

An adult cat needs around 400 g (14 oz) of food a day, spread over two or three meals. Don't give chocolate or encourage a sweet tooth in your pet.

P IS FOR POISONS

Keep puss out of the garage, where spilt oil or antifreeze could prove lethal. Other common substances, such as household cleaners, detergents, and paints, are all dangerous to the ever-curious cat. Many common houseplants are also poisonous and should be kept out of nibbling range.

Q IS FOR QUIET

All cats hate sudden loud noises, and a radio or hi-fi played at full blast can be painful to a cat's sensitive ears.

R IS FOR REPRODUCTION

Avoid the troubles of spraying, calling, and unwanted litters by making sure that all your cats are spayed or neutered by the time they are six months old.

S IS FOR SCRATCHING

A scratching post, tall enough for puss to stand on its hind legs and really dig in those claws, may discourage damage to furniture. But don't count on it!

T IS FOR TRAVEL

Carry puss in a well-ventilated, secure container that is easy to clean. On a long journey make regular stops for your cat to eat, drink, and use the litter tray. Never leave your cat unattended in a car, even if you will only be gone a short time.

U IS FOR
UPSET TUMMY
Cats will vomit easily for many reasons. Give puss no food for 12 hours, then offer a small meal. If no further vomiting occurs there is no need to worry. If at all anxious, however, or if the cat is listless or appears to be in pain, consult a vet immediately.

V IS FOR
VEGETABLES
Cooked or grated raw vegetables make a healthy addition to your cat's diet, but cats cannot live on a vegetarian diet: they need nutrients that are found only in meat. Make sure your pet has grass to chew, as this provides extra vitamins and also helps cats to regurgitate hairballs.

W IS FOR
WEANING
Kittens can be given some solid food in addition to milk when they are one month old. By two months, weaning will be complete.

X IS FOR
XPECTATIONS
It is perfectly reasonable to expect your cat to provide you with affection, companionship, and fun – but only if you honour your side of the bargain and give puss food, warmth, and plenty of loving care in return.

Y IS FOR YEAST
An occasional yeast tablet makes a crunchy treat and helps promote a healthy coat.

Z IS FOR ZOONOSES
A few feline complaints can be passed on to humans, but the risk is negligible provided cats are wormed regularly and owners observe good hygiene.

I N D E X

ACKNOWLEDGMENTS

Key: t=top; b=bottom; c=centre; l=left; r=right

DK Pictures
Jane Burton: 5, 37tr
Will Fowler: 13t
Steve Gorton and Tim Ridley: 16bl, 21t, 33t, 48, 49b, 54-55, 59
Marc Henrie: 8-9, 15, 18, 19tl, tc, cl, cr, bl, bc, br, 27, 29b, 32, 36, 49t, 57
*Dave King: 7, 16cl, br, 17tl, tr, cr, br, 19c, 20, 21 b, 22 /23, 24bl, 25t, 26,
28, 29t, 30-31, 33b, 34-35, 37bl, 38, 39, 41, 47, 50-51, 56*
Matthew Ward: 14, 17cl, 19tr, 46

Agency Pictures
Bridgeman Art Library: 11b
Mary Evans Pcture Library: 11t
Kobal Collection: 12, 13b
Popperfoto: 10

Design Assistance: *Patrizio Semproni*
Picture Research: *Diana Morris*
Illustration: *Susan Robertson, Stephen Lings, Clive Spong*

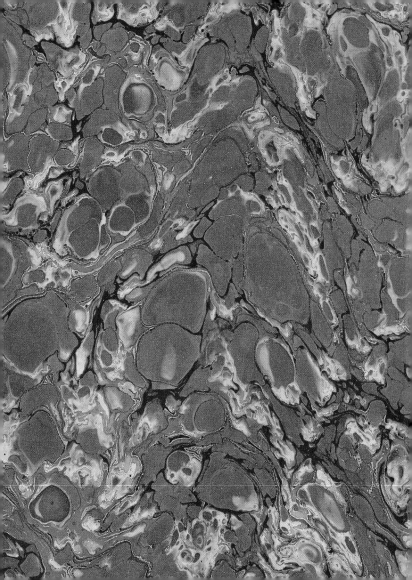